Handwriting Age 8–9

D1785295

Rhona Whiteford

Rhona Whiteford has many years' experience of teaching at preschool and primary school level, and is the author of a wide range of educational books for teachers, parents and children. She has two children.

Consultant: **Andrew Burrell**

Andrew Burrell has worked as a primary school teacher and as a lecturer at the Institute of Education, University of London, and has carried out research into the teaching of Language and Literacy.

Illustrated by **Tracey English**

About this book

This book contains handwriting activities suitable for 8- and 9-year-olds. They are based on the National Curriculum and National Literacy Strategy requirements for Year 4.

The activities gradually become more demanding, so it is important to start at the beginning.

The handwriting skills taught or practised in each unit are stated at the top of the page. A note at the foot of the page tells you more about the purpose of the activities and gives advice about how to help your child with them.

Stickers are provided as a reward and as a record, and the progress chart at the back of the book gives you a useful checklist of skills.

Each unit ends with a positive comment. Encouragement from you will work wonders, so be generous with your praise!

How to help your child

- Find a quiet place to work, preferably sitting at a table.

- Make sure your child has a sharp pencil. At this stage, you could introduce a good-quality fountain pen; a medium-width round nib, used with blue ink, will give a pleasing result.

- The pencil or pen should be held between the thumb and forefinger and supported by the middle finger.

- If your child is left-handed, turn the book slightly so that he or she can see the writing as it is formed.

- Encourage your child to check his or her work.

- Give opportunities for writing notes and lists in everyday life.

Above all, be relaxed – and have fun!

Hodder Children's Books
a division of
Hodder Headline Limited

My best writing

I'm Poppy, and I'm going to help you to write really well!

Copy the text in your best handwriting.

FUN

ACTIVITIES FOR CHILDREN

INTERESTING

my bestseller

my match-winning racket

swimming
riding
football
skating
skiing
reading
art
modelling
tennis
cycling
rugby
cooking
cricket
dancing
music
collecting

my record-breaking skateboard

my latest hit

You can have fun with many kinds of activity.

There are speedy ones which needs wheels, balls or water.

Some, like reading or painting, are less energetic.

What's your favourite?

Four activities I'd like to try

Encourage your child to concentrate, and to maintain a rhythm as he writes.

Use this page as a yardstick for assessing his handwriting again at the end of the book.

2

Brilliant!

Warming up

In medieval times, people enjoyed decorating things with patterns.

Complete each of these writing patterns in the correct colour.

Pattern practice will help your child to control the pen and to develop a rhythm.

The patterns should be evenly spaced and made with firm strokes. Encourage your child to use colour and to take a pride in the appearance of his work.

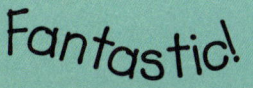

Fantastic!

3

Writing with a slope

It is easier to write quickly if you slope your writing like this.

Practise these sloping patterns.

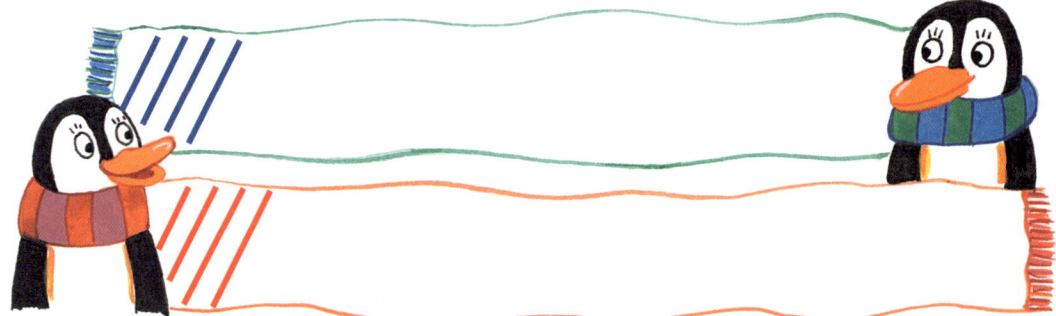

Poppy

Now practise writing letters and numerals with a slope.

abcdefghijklmn opqrstuvwxyz

1 2 3 4 5 6 7 8 9 0

A B C D E F G

H I J K L M N

O P Q R S T U

V W X Y Z

By this stage, your child should be comfortable with upright joined writing and ready to learn how to write with a slope. This will make it easier for her to write quickly and fluently.

Sloping unjoined letters are practised on these two pages. The writing should slope forwards slightly, and the spaces between letters and words should be the same as in upright writing.

Try sloping your paper like this.

Left-handed

Right-handed

Now label these.

Write your own name and the names of friends or family members.

Use unjoined letters, and remember to slope your writing.

's

ROOM

This book belongs to

Maths

's

DIARY

KEEP OUT

Signed:

This activity allows your child to try sloped writing in a practical context. The slope should be consistent, and she could practise in pencil before completing the page in ink.

Look at the illustration at the top of the page, which shows paper position for left- and right-handers. (Some left-handers have a tendency to slope their writing backwards, and this should be corrected as early as possible.)

Interesting!

Letter sets; Join 1

Don't forget to slope your writing!

These are the letter **sets**.

Set 1
acdeh
iklm
nstu

Set 2
acdegijm
nopqrs
uvwxy

Set 3
bfh
klt

Set 4
forvw

Join 1
can join

any letter in **Set 1**

to

any letter in **Set 2**

Practise Join 1.

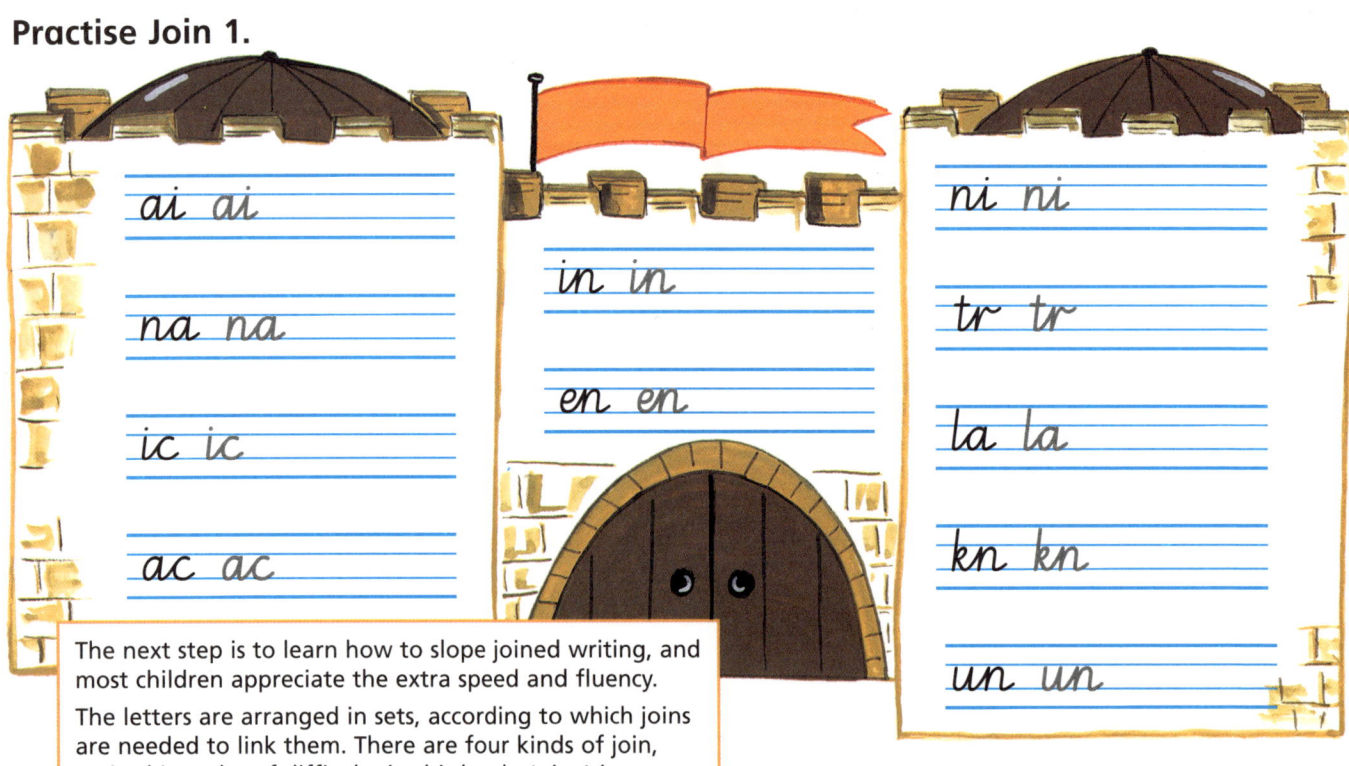

ai ai

na na

ic ic

ac ac

in in

en en

ni ni

tr tr

la la

kn kn

un un

The next step is to learn how to slope joined writing, and most children appreciate the extra speed and fluency.

The letters are arranged in sets, according to which joins are needed to link them. There are four kinds of join, revised in order of difficulty in this book. Join 1 is a diagonal join, going from the baseline to the top of the next letter. The pairs of letters on this page can be found in common words such as *main*, *knee* and *end*.

Well done!

Join 2

Join 2 can join

Set 1
a c d e h
i k l m
n s t u

any letter in **Set 1**

at

to

Set 3
b f h
k l t

any letter in **Set 3**

Practise Join 2.

ch ch

th th

ck ck

al al

ll ll

ab ab

uf uf

af af

ef ef

ut ut

When joining to *f* or *t*, don't make the join too spread out.

Take that to the cat!

That cat?

I'll eat my hat!

The second join is also a diagonal join, going from the baseline to the top of an ascender. The pairs of letters on this page can be found in common words such as *luck*, *such* and *this*.

Excellent!

7

Join 3

Join 3 can join

Set 4

*for
v w*

any letter in **Set 4**

og

to

Set 2

*a c d e g i
j m n o p q r
s u v w x y*

any letter in **Set 2**

Practise Join 3.

oa oa	wi wi	og og
rd rd	ox ox	fe fe
os os	ve ve	fa fa

Help is here!

The letter *e* changes its shape according to which letter it follows.

Join 1 to *e*

me me

Join 3 to *e*

we we

The third join is a horizontal join which goes from the top of one letter to the top of the next. The pairs of letters on this page can be found in common words such as *win*, *dog* and *vet*.

Make sure that your child does not make the curve of the join too long, as this will leave too much space between the letters.

8

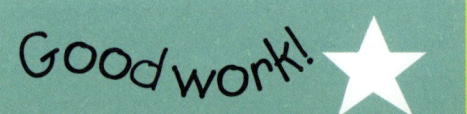

Join 4

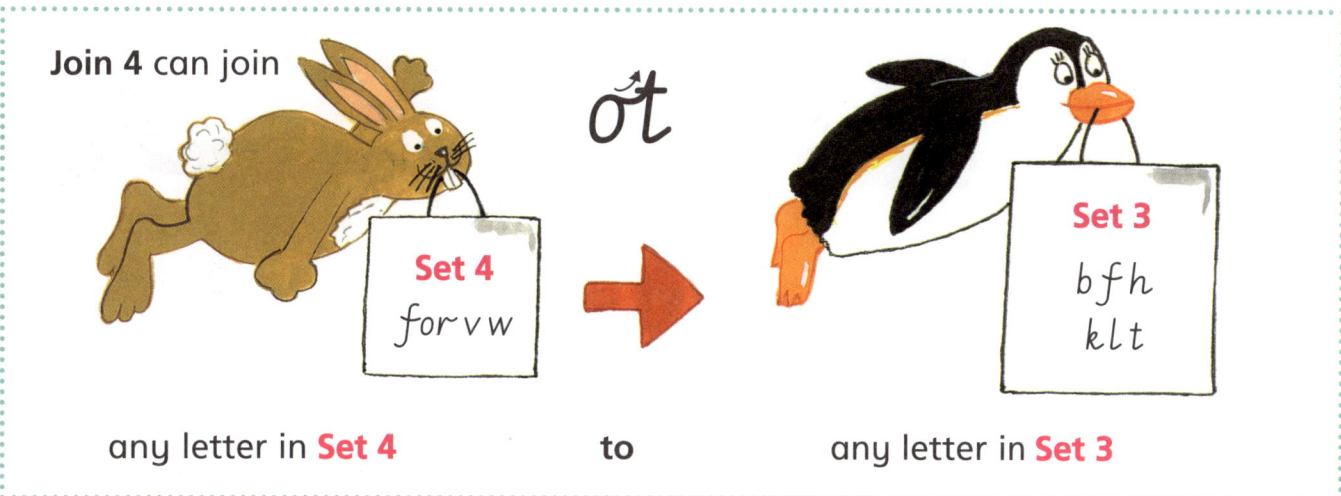

Join 4 can join

Set 4
for v w

any letter in **Set 4**   **to**   any letter in **Set 3**

o⃗t

Set 3
b f h
k l t

Practise Join 4.

wh wh

ot ot

oh oh

wl wl

ft ft

rb rb

ft ft

of of

ff ff

Look! Is that a whale?

No, it's lots of newts doing the crawl!

The fourth join goes from the top of one letter to the top of the ascender of the next. The pairs of letters on this page can be found in common words such as *off*, *what* and *when*.

Make sure that the upstroke of the join is made at a tight angle. Remind your child to rest the heel of her hand on the paper, stretching her fingers to form the ascenders.

Wonderful! ★

The breakaway letters

The breakaway letters
b g j p
q x y z

These eight letters are not followed by a join.
They are called the **breakaway letters**.

No join is made to or from z.

Practise the breakaway letters. Match each pet to its owner.

PET SHOW

Pets	Owners
Bobby Bomber	Maxine Wax
Dippy Dodger	Roger Badger
Quackquack	Sam Sizzle
Gonzo Goggle	Peggy Pippin
Jelly Jambo	Crazy Maisie

In some handwriting schemes, some of these eight letters are followed by a join. Check your child's school style, to avoid confusion.

Brilliant!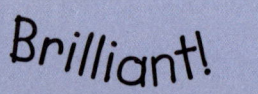

Capitals in capitals

Copy the names of the capital cities.

ROME

BELFAST

DUBLIN

PARIS

WASHINGTON D.C.

BRUSSELS

LONDON

CARDIFF

BERLIN

EDINBURGH

Capital letters are never joined!

All the capital letters are the same height, and none has a descender (tail). Some are composed of straight lines only, while others contain curves. Encourage your child to make the straight lines with firm strokes and to form well-rounded curves.

Fantastic!

11

Poems and rhymes

Poems by a penguin!

Look at the layout of these two poems.
Copy one of them in your joined, sloping handwriting.

The otter
The otter's a little
    Like a cat.
He's sleek and polished,
    Never fat!
He's quick when ghostly
    Moonbeams dart,
Out on his business,
    Quick, and smart.

Steel lines
A spider weaves a web
    That's tight.
It holds the roof down
    In the night.
It's fine as silver,
    Strong as steel
And she lets it out
    Like a fishing reel.

Point out the fact that each line of these poems begins with a capital letter, with every other line indented. Encourage your child to remember a line at a time as she writes. This will help her to write rhythmically without breaking off to look at the words she is copying.

Now try these limericks.

There was a young girl from mid-Lancs,
Who got up to some terrible pranks;
    She shampooed the cat,
    Spread glue on the mat,
And blocked up the door with old planks.

A sea-serpent saw a big tanker,
Bit a hole in her side and then sank her,
    He swallowed the crew
    In a minute or two,
And then picked his teeth with the anchor.

Anon

All limericks have five lines, and here
the two shortest lines are indented.

Remind your child to concentrate on
sloping her writing and to keep the
spaces between words the same length.

Very fluent! ★

13

Spelling patterns

Practising letter patterns will make you a good speller!

Practise these spelling patterns.

right light	ight ight
caught taught	aught aught
bought fought	ought ought
walking singing	ing ing
babies ladies	ies ies
looked cooked	ed ed
heavier busier	ier ier
heaviest busiest	iest iest

The letter patterns on these two pages occur at the ends of many words in English. Practising them will help your child with spelling as well as handwriting, as his hand will learn to form the patterns automatically.

14

Race to the place where the word is!

fully   carefully

ness   happiness

ship   friendship

hood   brotherhood

ment   statement

ary   secondary

ify   petrify

ate   decorate

Think of more words which end with these letter patterns, and help your child to learn them.

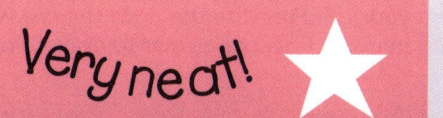

Very neat!

The print style

Print letters are very plain, and they do not join.

We use the print style when we need to write very clearly.

Here are the lower case print letters. Copy them carefully.

a b c d e f g h i j k l m n o p q r s t u v w x y z

Copy Poppy's name.

Poppy Prunella Penguin

The capital letters are the same as the ones you have already learned.

Label these keys with the names of friends or family members.

Printing is a plain, unjoined style. It is useful for writing which needs to be very clear, such as labelling. Some children find it difficult to stop joining once they have started, and you may wish to let your child practise the print style by writing labels for her possessions or for household items. Let her use a ruler to draw faint pencil guidelines if necessary.

Remember not to slope the print letters!

Now fill in this form, using neat print.
Write your own details, or pretend you are a story character.

PERSONAL FILE   Date ....

Name .... Date of birth ....

Address ....

....

....

Interests 1 ....

        2 ....

        3 ....

Hair colour .... Eye colour ....

Distinguishing features ....

....

School ....

Main achievements to date ....

....

Future plans ....

....

                        Signature: ....

Involve your child when you are filling in a real form, showing her the difference between the completed and uncompleted versions. As with all styles of writing, print letters and words should be evenly spaced.

Well done!

Label this map using clear print.

Make sure your writing fits the space!

BANE ISLAND   Viper Inlet   Wailing Marsh

Ocean Caverns   Forest of Fear   Quivering Sands

Creeping Cliffs   Goodman's Wreck   Totem

Boiling Pit   Volcano Bay

Old Jimbo Dreadnought

Let your child label the map using fine rollerball or fibre-tipped pens in different colours. Look at road maps together, comparing the styles of print.

You could use capital letters!

Complete this party invitation and the reply slip.
Use print or joined writing, or a combination.

Invitation

to ....'s party

to celebrate ....

Please wear ....

It's at ....

Starting at .... Date ....

R.S.V.P. Tel. .... From ....

Reply slip

Dear ....

I would .... to come.

I'm going to wear ....

From ....

★ Tel. .... Special message ....

Excellent! ★

Riddles

Pick up a pen for a penguin!

Read these riddles, and copy the punchlines in your best joined writing.

What's the best birthday present?
Difficult question, but a drum takes a lot of beating!

....

What song was sung when the yacht exploded?
Pop goes the wee sail!

....

What's the most unfortunate letter in the alphabet?
The letter u – it's always in trouble !

....

Why is the letter e lazy?
Because it's always in bed!

What's the end of
everything?
The letter g!

....

Why is an island like the letter t?
Because it's in the middle of water!

....

In a word containing an apostrophe (e.g. *what's, you'll*),
the letter following the apostrophe is not joined to the
previous letter. Point this out to your child.

20

Read these riddles, and write the correct piece of speech in each speech bubble.

Boy: *Where does a lamb go for a haircut?*

Girl: *To a baa baa shop!*

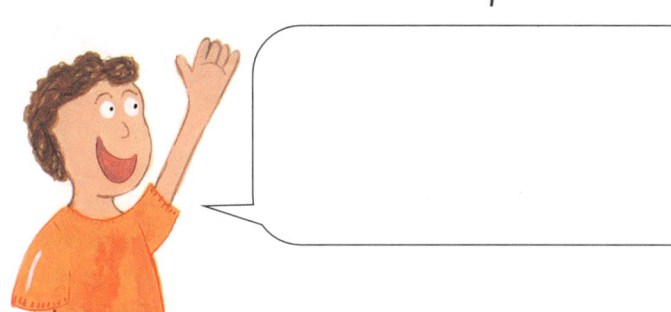

Girl: *What do you call a bull asleep on the ground?*

Boy: *A bulldozer!*

Now write this riddle as a piece of dialogue.

How do you catch a squirrel?

Climb a tree and act like a nut!

Girl: ....

Squirrel: ....

Good work! ⭐

Making an impact

Look at the shape of the poem. It helps us to enjoy the words.

Copy this poem carefully.

Lightning cracks the
heavens apart –
White knives
tearing at a sky   that's dark,
Jagged rips as the
clouds crash down,
Covering mountains,
fields
and towns.

This is a shape poem, or a concrete poem. Find ideas for shape poems in poetry books, or think them up together. You could try writing a 'rain' poem in the shape of an umbrella, or a 'sun' poem in the shape of the sun.

Ask your helper to read each of these words aloud.
What sort of picture comes to mind?
Look at the word.
Does it look like your mind picture?

shine BOOM blood wobble wiggle

Now write each of these words in suitable lettering.

You can use joined writing, print, capital letters – whatever you like!

slither

sunny

crack

crisp

strong

shaky

A word written in a lettering style that suits its meaning is called a calligram. Talk about each of the words on this page, and help your child to decide which style of lettering to use. For example, *shaky* could be written in wobbly letters, and *crack* could be written in broken letters.

Wonderful! ★

Writing a passage

Writing long passages develops a good rhythm.

Copy this passage in your best joined handwriting.

The desert can be an interesting place. During the day the sun blazes down on the scorched sands. You may see the odd group of travellers on camels, but there are few other animals apart from reptiles.

The desert night is cold and dark, and plants such as cacti and grasses get water from moisture in the air. You could see the fennec fox and the desert rat, a relative of the pet gerbil. There are tarantulas, too.

Continuous narrative is usually written in lower case letters (with capitals where needed) as this makes it easy to read.

Let your child place a ruler or a strip of paper under the line being copied, to keep her place. To help her to write without guidelines, show her how to make small pencil marks at regular intervals down the left-hand side of the writing space. These can be used as starting points, and will help her to keep even spaces between the lines.

Brilliant!

Lists

Some lists need to be written quickly and then thrown away.

Some lists are kept for a long time.

This is my quick list!

Copy this list quickly.
Use joined writing.

> Needed for Christmas
> Present for ....
> Present for ....
> Wrapping paper
> Gift tags
> Ribbon

Now copy this list using neat print.
Tick the items you would like!

> Useful things for any schoolchild
> Self-sharpening pencil
> Homing eraser
> Daily supply of invisible sweets
> Wrist TV

Encourage your child to illustrate or decorate the second list. Suggest that she makes a personal 'wish list', decorating it with gold and silver marker pens.

Involve your child when you are making a list. You could dictate a shopping list, speaking fairly quickly so that she will need to practise speed writing.

Very quick!

Messages

Copy each of these messages and then write one of your own.
Use capital letters, print script and joined writing.

A fridge magnet

CHILL OUT

A message in a bottle

I'm shipwrecked on the
blue island south of Fiji.
My windsurfer was
off-course.
Help, please!

Some crackers
have jokes or riddles
in them!

A message in a cracker

The less we speak,
the more we hear!

The activity asks your child to write a variety
of very brief messages in appropriate styles.

Write real messages, and leave them around
the home for each other to find.

Letters

Handwritten letters are written in joined writing. They are laid out like this:

Name and address of the person you are writing to →

Leave a margin →

Mr. Wolf
The Pit in the Woods
Black Valley
Farshire

The Dell
Misty Mount
Farshire OAK 123

Tel. Farshire Tree Tree Tree

1st August 2001

← Your address

← Your phone number

← Today's date

Start here →

Dear Mr. Wolf

I am writing to tell you that the Forest Rangers have had enough of your activities. Lurking behind trees and stealing from picnics is no way to make a living! We are especially cross about your treatment of Miss Riding Hood and the destruction of local pigs' houses. Please mend your ways, or we will evict you from the Pit!

Yours sincerely

Sign off here →

Roger the Ranger

Your name →

Forest Headquarters

Copy the letter on a sheet of paper, or make up a similar one.

Look at the layout of the letter together, and help your child to copy it neatly and accurately.

Look at some real letters together; try to find a variety including handwritten personal letters and typed business letters.

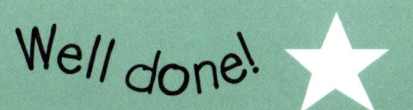

Well done!

A magic spell

Decorate the borders of the spell.

**Copy this spell in your best joined writing.
Use a fountain pen.**

Take a broken clock (squashed by a rock),

And a blob of ink with goo from the sink.

Put this in a dish with a smelly old fish

And an old school dinner (tears make it thinner).

Whizz it all up by the light of the moon,

Better be quick, speed up, make it soon!

Smear the stuff on teacher's chair

And watch her vanish, from toes to hair!

Show your child how to mark the starting point for each line, and help her to judge how big her writing should be (small enough to fit the spaces but large enough to be legible). Remind her to make the ascenders and descenders long enough.

Excellent!

Speed writing

Sometimes speed is necessary!

Copy these proverbs as fast as you can in joined writing.

Live and let live.

....

A bird in the hand is worth two in the bush.

....

....

Many hands make light work.

....

Let sleeping dogs lie.

....

Make hay while the sun shines.

....

Strike while the iron's hot.

....

How many proverbs can you write in one minute?

Empty vessels make the most noise.

....

How long does it take you to write all eight proverbs as fast as you can?

Actions speak louder than words.

....

minutes   seconds

Time your child as she writes one of the proverbs, and see whether she can increase her speed without losing legibility.

Good work! ★

29

More labels

Label these school books in neat print.
Use capital letters for the titles.

Book Titles

Football tips	Puzzles
Creepy crawlies	Favourite sums
Your bicycle	Rocks and stones
Furry animals	All Sports

Children's names

Sarah Snorkel	Ali Anteater
Jemma Jelly	Milly Mango
Emily Egg	Oliver Ostrich
Tom Tuff	

Jemma Jelly
ALL SPORTS

Let your child use a fountain pen or fine felt-tipped pens for this activity.

Many labels need to be quite small. Encourage him to judge the size and spacing of his writing by eye; he will get better at this with practice.

Copy the advertisement and the labels in neat print.

FRUIT ICE LOLLY MAKER

FROM FRUIT TO FROZEN IN 10 MINUTES

Fruit chute

Cooler controls

Power

Portable power pack

Water wash-in

Stick input

Ice-out

Crazy conveyor

Penguins pick ice pops!

Wonderful! ⭐

Skills test

Write the names of your ten favourite people and places.
Use a fountain pen, and your best joined writing.

Decorate the borders!

People

···························
···························
···························
···························
···························
···························
···························
···························
···························
···························

Places

···························
···························
···························
···························
···························
···························
···························
···························
···························
···························

Has your handwriting improved?

This page gives you the opportunity to assess your child's handwriting after the practice provided in this book. Compare her handwriting with that on page 2, allowing for the fact that a slope should now be evident. Look for well formed letters and joins, even spaces between letters and words, and a consistent angle of slope.

Even better! ★